When God Gets Angry with a Nation

David R. Mains

Sept - 1985

David C. Cook Publishing Co.
ELGIN, ILLINOIS—WESTON, ONTARIO

All Scripture quotations are from the Revised Standard Version
unless otherwise noted.

Published by David C. Cook Publishing Co., Elgin, IL 60120
Cover design by Joe Ragont
Printed in the United States of America.
ISBN 0-89191-263-0
LC 80-51281

CONTENTS

The Chapel Talks Series
by David Mains

Making Church More Enjoyable
How to Support Your Pastor
How to Resist Temptation
God, Help Us with the Kids
What's Wrong with Lukewarm?
Praying More Effectively
Getting to Know the Holy Spirit
When God Gets Angry with a Nation
A Closer Walk with God
Psalms That Touch Us Where We Live
Making Scripture Yours
I Needed That Encouragement

Introduction

Most people listen to the radio while they're doing something else. As a broadcaster I'm aware that a person hearing me is probably shaving, fixing breakfast, driving to work, or some similar activity. Being able to keep his or her attention in such a setting is a lot different than preaching to a captive audience.

Therefore, I was dubious as to whether the slow pace of radio with its need for frequent repetition and underscoring each key truth would transfer all that well into print.

To complicate matters further, every time a program is made I must assume many listeners didn't hear what was said the day before. But just the opposite is true when compiling the chapters of a book. They build on one another.

Well, the first series of Chapel talks is now completed. Through the help of others, my broadcast scripts have been made more readable than I thought possible. The greatest thanks for this project goes to my wife, Karen, who put aside her own writing to help me out. Two Chapel of the Air staff members, Ruby Christian and Sharon Morse, also did yeoman duty typing long hours after work and on weekends.

As you read through this book I would strongly recommend studying the biblical material designated in each chapter heading.

1

NOT AS BAD
AS THEY ARE
Amos 1—2

How would you react if you heard a Mexican citizen preaching on our American streets: "For multiplied transgressions, the Lord will no longer revoke punishment of the Soviet Union. For the imprisonment and murder, in our lifetime, of countless innocent victims, God will send fire upon Moscow!

"For similar atrocities, practiced time and again, very soon China will also receive just recompense from the Lord.

"Hear next what has been revealed to me concerning the Arab nations. For their inhumanities, payment will surely be extracted from them."

If you can imagine such a messenger, including his English broken by a thick Spanish accent, you'll have a feel anyway, of how the prophet Amos must have appeared about 760 years before Christ. Amos came from southern Judah, an independent nation that was part of a split in Solomon's kingdom following his death almost 200 years earlier.

Amos stood in Samaria, the capital of the ten stronger northern tribes, and instead of predicting troubles ahead for Russia, China, and the Arab countries, he prophesied doom for Syria (immediately to the north); on Tyre (Phoenicia) in the northwest; and Philistia on the west coast. This was not just a catchy introduction, although I'm sure what he said attracted the attention of his hearers. What Amos predicted would come to pass.

"Thus says the Lord," the doomsayer continued, "for three transgressions, and for four" (another way of saying multiplied offenses), a second cluster of nations faces trouble." This time the offenders were even nearer home and each was related in some way to Israel: Edom, where the descendants of Esau, Jacob's brother, lived; and Ammon and Moab, whose people stemmed from the sons of Lot, the nephew of Abraham.

When you take time to read Amos 1-2 you'll find that the basic sin cited against each country thus far was the practice of inhumane, heartless, savage acts. The Edomites pursued brothers "with the sword, and cast off all pity" (1:11). The people of Ammon "ripped up women with child in Gilead" (1:13) and so on.

"Thus says the Lord," and now he talks about Judah, "I will not revoke the punishment" (2:4). (He can't get any closer to Israel than Judah!) God will "devour the strongholds of Jerusalem" (2:5) because they rejected the law of the Lord (2:4). Maybe you noticed that the reason for punishment has now shifted.

But more in question at the moment is whether or not

this uninvited shepherd, wandering out of Tekoa in southern Judah, will have sense enough to stop his mouth or will he now raise accusations against Israel herself? The narration continues in Amos 2:6: God says, "For three transgressions of Israel, and for four, I will not revoke the punishment." And now the remainder of the book, seven and a half chapters, is about the sins of the nation to which Amos has come to preach.

Maybe it would be good to sketch in some background. If ever there was a time when Israel seemed invulnerable, it was now. The long reign of Jeroboam II had been extremely prosperous. The boundaries of the nation extended farther than at any period since the days of Solomon himself. So what gave this presumptuous shepherd/preacher from Israel's weaker southern adversary, Judah, the right to speak ridiculous annunciations?

The Lord says "I raised up some of your sons for prophets, and some of your young men for Nazirites. Is it not indeed so, O people of Israel? . . .

But you made the Nazirites drink wine, and commanded the prophets, saying, 'You shall not prophesy.'

Behold, I will press you down in your place, as a cart full of sheaves presses down. Flight shall perish from the swift, and the strong shall not retain his strength, nor shall the mighty save his life; he who handles the bow shall not stand, and he who is swift of foot shall not save himself, nor shall he who rides the horse save his life; and he who is stout of heart among the mighty shall flee away naked in that day," says the Lord (2:11-16).

Why? Because Israel had sold the righteous for silver, and the needy for a pair of shoes (2:6). Amos is preaching against the greed of the unrighteous officials of the city who could be bought off for silver, or who for as paltry a debt as a pair of shoes would turn over a man to be a slave to his creditors.

They trampled the head of the poor into the dust and turned aside the way of the afflicted (2:7). "A man and his father go in to the same maiden, so my holy name is profaned; they lay themselves down beside every altar upon garments taken in pledge" (vv. 7-8).

That needs explaining. Israel's law said that a poor man who was obliged to pawn his outer garment was to have it returned to him before night. Exodus 22:26, 27 reads: "If ever you take your neighbor's garment in pledge, you shall restore it to him before the sun goes down; for that is his only covering, it is his mantle for his body; in what else shall he sleep? And if he cries to me, I will hear, for I am compassionate." Deuteronomy 24:12, 13 reemphasizes the principle: "And if he is a poor man, you shall not sleep in his pledge; when the sun goes down, you shall restore to him the pledge that he may sleep in his cloak and bless you; and it shall be righteousness to you before the Lord your God." Amos points to the violation of this compassionate legality.

The sermon rolls on. "In the house of their God they drank the wine of those who have been fined" (Amos 2:8). In other words, these people were getting drunk on wine purchased with money gained by unjust levys, and the offense was happening in the very house of their God, because the prophet was talking about the sacred places of Israel set up at Bethel and Dan.

Amos further developed the theme of Israel's sins in the sermons yet to be studied, but already he's wagged his finger at the injustices of bribe taking on the part of the leaders, contempt for the poor and the powerless, immoral sexual practices, profaned worship and drunkenness. Because of these, God's judgment was invoked against Israel.

Though less cruel than other nations, a wicked people with godly roots should expect drastic divine punishment.* In a sentence, that's Amos' opening message.

As incredible as his words must have seemed at the moment of delivery, within about forty years Israel would be so defeated and humiliated and scattered by the Assyrians it would be impossible even to trace her people. The ten lost tribes of Israel would be the name given them and the northern kingdom would become the classic illustration for ultimate dispersion and assimilation. Scary, isn't it?

The prophets who witnessed the demise of the northern kingdom in the eighth century before Christ have an uncanny relevance to our own times. Amos sounded the earliest note of warning. With a broken heart, Hosea next told the people of God's unreturned love. Next came Micah, then the marvelously literate prophecies of Isaiah.

I want you to begin reading this short book of Amos. It's too easy to substitute commentaries for the actual study of Scriptures. Explore Amos, with the Bible as your primary source and this book only as an aid.

Look for applications, but don't jump to conclusions. The parallels are not immediately obvious. For example,

I don't think that the taking of bribes by our officials is widespread the way it was in the time when Amos preached. Neither is American society as heartless regarding the poor. Possibly we're approaching ancient Israel in terms of sexual impurity. Drunkenness—that's a major problem, too! The mixing of true worship with false intrusions—we could have quite a discussion about that.

God doesn't judge all nations by the same standard. From Amos 1-2 we know that his divine expectations differ. People with godly roots shouldn't expect to be exempted from punishment just because their wickedness is not as great as that of godless neighbors.

Yes, America is less cruel than many contemporary world powers. To argue such a point is hardly necessary. Without question, as a people, we have been blessed with a most unique godly heritage. I do not say we are a Christian nation, but the contribution of the church to our national life in days past has been significant indeed.

Unfortunately, at this present time we are also a wicked people. Not just because I say so—listen to our music, observe the violence that fills our news reports, study the divorce percentages, poll the rest of the world for their opinions. More than that, walk close to God and have him burden your heart regarding the growing sin of this land.

Then remember from Scripture the opening point of the prophet Amos, *Though less cruel than other nations, a wicked people with godly roots should expect drastic divine punishment.*

2

MY CHILDREN SHOULD KNOW BETTER
Amos 3

How would you like being a citizen of a nation obviously blessed by God in a unique fashion? What if the Almighty himself said about your country—"You only have I known of all the families of the earth." Would that make you feel good?

Do you think God would be more or less tolerant of sins committed among such an honored people? Would the advantage of godly closeness indicate immunity from punishment for wrongdoing? Like some overly indulgent parent, might God be excessively lenient when it came to correcting the flaws of those he cares about so greatly?

The prophet Amos hit this issue head on in a sermon preached three quarters of a millennium before the time of Christ. At that point in history, the Jewish tribes had been split into separate kingdoms for about two hundred years. Amos hailed from little Tekoa in Judah, the name given the nation composed of the two southern tribes. he was preaching uninvited in Israel, the name which referred to the ten northern tribes where Jeroboam II ruled from his capital city of Samaria.

From all outward appearances, the good hand of the Lord still rested upon Israel. Her boundaries stretched farther than at any period since Solomon had been monarch over a unified people. Had not Damascus, to the immediate north, been defeated? Wasn't powerful Assyria, farther north and east, too distant and occupied with internal struggles to be of any threat?

With the menace of war removed, the caravan trains now brought the country wealth and culture. Unfortunately, along with prosperity came greed and dishonesty, violence and drunkenness, corruption on the part of officials, and heightened participation in sexual excesses. Great divisions marked the haves and the have nots; the poor were not only ignored, they were ruthlessly exploited. Underneath all this was a base of spiritual travesty. Many years earlier this northern kingdom had set up in both Bethel and Dan, the two religious centers, a golden calf to symbolize Jehovah. Now, in addition, and probably as a consequence, degenerate religious cults flourished throughout Israel.

"Hear this word that the Lord has spoken against you, O people of Israel," thundered Amos, "against the whole family which I brought up out of the land of Egypt: 'You only have I known of all the families of the earth; therefore I will punish you for all your iniquities'" (Amos 3:1-2).

Well, there's Amos' answer to my earlier inquiry. Abused privileges bring stricter discipline! The very reason God is going to chastise Israel is precisely because of the great honor he had bestowed on her.

Amos continued:

Proclaim to the strongholds in Assyria, and to the strongholds in the land of Egypt [these were the two opposing super powers, one to the northeast of Israel and the other to the southwest], and say, "Assemble yourselves upon the mountains of Samaria, and see the great tumults within her [how everything is turned upside down!], and the oppressions in her midst. They do not know how to do right," says the LORD, "those who store up violence and robbery in their strongholds (vv. 9-10).

On the day I punish Israel for his transgressions, I will punish the altars of Bethel, [that's where one of the calves stood; Bethel was the northern kingdom's equivalent to the temple in Jerusalem] and the horns of the altar shall be cut off and fall to the ground. I will smite the winter house with the summer house; and the houses of ivory shall perish, and the great houses shall come to an end," says the Lord (vv. 14, 15). That's a blast at the luxury of the wealthy, who have dishonestly gained their opulence at the expense of the poor.

Notice the extreme of the destruction Amos forecast, and remember that he was a shepherd. "Thus says the Lord: 'As the shepherd rescues from the mouth of the lion two legs, or a piece of an ear, so shall the people of Israel who dwell in Samaria be rescued, with the corner of a couch and part of a bed'" (v. 12). In other words, he's saying, "There won't be much left, folks!"

Now I presume these words got a certain number of laughs. Fulfillment of such horrors seemed impossible. Maybe some hearers jeered. Probably most didn't take Amos seriously, but within just forty years, Assyria, a nation many historians consider the most cruel in the history of the world, would sweep down upon Israel. Viewing the remains of their ruthless violence, I'm sure some people would look back and say, "You know, old Amos got it right! There's not much left here but an ear and two legs that already have been pretty well gnawed!"

Have you ever heard of the ten lost tribes of Israel? This is the historical culmination from which that term comes. There was nothing remaining of which to speak. Numbers would squirm to death, impaled on sharp stakes driven through their chests, as was the Assyrian custom. Less than 28,000 went into exile—so scattered they couldn't be traced. Foreigners imported into the conquered territory would intermarry with the humiliated survivors and be called Samaritans, the half-Jews against whom the Hebrew people of Christ's time were so bigoted.

The thrust of the word delivered by Amos in chapter 3 is: *The privilege of God's favor inherently contains the promise of greater punishment for evils committed.*

Whether Israel was ready to hear it or not, Amos continued to preach (vv. 4-8), "Does a lion roar in the forest, when he has no prey? . . . Surely the Lord God does nothing, without revealing his secret to his servants the prophets. The lion has roared; who will not fear?

The Lord God has spoken; who can but prophesy?'"
And the Lord has spoken against you saying, "'Of all the
families of the earth you only have I known; therefore I
will punish you for all your iniquities.'"

Now I can't say why God has burdened me to review
the prophets of the eighth century before Christ, but I
have been strongly drawn to Amos, Hosea, Micah, and
Isaiah, the men who witnessed the demise of Israel. I'm
not even yet certain how the events of these final years
of the northern kingdom relate to us. But I do have that
strong sense of the Lord leading me as I started in this
direction.

Is it because America is like ancient Israel? In some
ways, yes; in others, no. Certainly the unique promises
made to Abraham and his children were never given to
America. As a people, we have not walked on dry land
through a sea, or been led by a divine cloud during the
day or a pillar of fire by night. Neither is our government
theocratic.

Yet the good hand of God has rested upon this land
far beyond what most nations have experienced. No,
I'm not confusing "divine endowments" with territories
taken from Indians. Nor do I see our wealth as coming
all from God, neither am I ignoring the fact that we have
often taken advantage of the resources of undeveloped
lands. Granted, it is a complex study to evaluate
accurately all that contributes to American life as we
know it.

Nevertheless, I believe there remains much truth in
the song, "America, America, God shed His grace on
thee." A significant part of the story of this land has been
and always will be centered on the relationship of our

people to the living Christ. In fact, looking at the earth today, I believe in many ways God could rightly say to us, "Of all the families of the earth, you have I known in a special way!"

Do we then assume that this love will blind him to trespasses that mark us as a people? Like northern Israel, do we shrug off warnings which insist the most important factor in terms of our future is whether or not God is pleased with how we live? Even if such talk seems a thousand miles from reality, nevertheless, it's true!

So be reminded, America, that favor with God inherently carries with it even greater punishment for evil committed. Did not our Lord himself say (Luke 12:48), "Everyone to whom much is given, of him will much be required"?

What is the future for a land that openly defies God's sexual standards? That no longer frowns on taking his holy name in vain? That seems incapable of controlling personal greed, even with frequent comparisons to the rest of a needy world? That has a vociferous appetite for violence in what it calls informative news reports and entertainment? That more and more pushes God out of its world view because of a discomfort with the mystery of his spiritual presence in all of life? That capitulates to unstable patterns of cohabitation because of its inability to keep its marriages and families intact? That has staggering percentages of people bound to debilitating habits such as alcohol and drugs? That wastes hours of time being entertained with trivia while world enemies plan its downfall?

You be the prophet! What is the future for such a land? As you answer, remember all the spiritual advantages she has known throughout her time!

Israel! Be reminded and repent. That was the message of Amos that went unheeded.

Does America need to hear the same words?

How will she respond?

3

UNHEEDED WARNING SIGNS
Amos 4

I don't know whether or not Amos would temper his remarks to women were he to address them in this feminist-conscious day, but back in time about 750 years before Christ he called the wealthy wives in Israel "fat cows"! Actually, the way it reads is, "Hear this word, you cows of Bashan" (Amos 4:1). Cows from that territory, however, were known for their fatness.

If his language was strong, the offenses of those addressed were great as well. They are those "who oppress the poor," he continued, "who crush the needy, who say to their husbands, 'Bring, that we may drink!'"

At the time of this sermonizing, the kingdom of Israel was in an extremely backslidden state. Though prosperous and militarily strong, cultural advantages were enjoyed by only the few. The poor were not only neglected (chaps. 1-3), but actually exploited. In this passage, Amos rails against the wives of the unjust officials who instead of being troubled in conscience over how their wealth had been gained, actually agreed with their dishonest husbands, demanding, "Bring more drink. After all, are we not the elite of this land?"

In chapter 6 Amos is more specific regarding this class of people when he prophesies, "Woe to those who lie upon beds of ivory . . ., eat lambs from the flock . . ., sing idle songs . . ., drink wine in bowls, and anoint themselves with the finest oils, but are not grieved over the ruin of Joseph! Therefore they shall now be the first of these to go into exile, and the revelry . . . shall pass away" (vv. 4-7).

Back in chapter 4, Amos is more pointed regarding the fate of these women. "The Lord God has sworn by his holiness that, behold, the days are coming upon you, they shall take you away with hooks, even the last of you with fishhooks" (v. 2). He's saying, liked animals led with hooks through their noses or fish picked up by hooks in their mouths, so you will be taken prisoner from here literally with hooks. It wasn't a pretty picture when painted prophetically, and it looked no better when it later came true.

Because the text shifts in emphasis I will return to verses 1-3 in my final chapter of this book. At the moment it's enough to report that selfish, hardened, calloused women is another condition to add to the list of sins uninvited Amos has been preaching against. Evils he's already enumerated were the dishonest judges, drunkenness, oppression of the poor, sexual perversions, violence, and, of course, a sterile religion.

Yes, the people in Israel still went through the forms of worship, but the heart of their faith had been destroyed. After all, had they not for years defied the firmest of their prohibitions and symbolized Jehovah as a golden calf?

"Come to Bethel, and transgress" (v. 4). Already we know these words of Amos are sarcastic. That's like inviting people to attend church to sin. "'Come to Bethel, and transgress; . . . bring your sacrifices every morning . . ., proclaim freewill offerings, publish them; for so you love to do, O people of Israel!' says the Lord God" (vv. 4-5).

Now the real heart of Amos' prophecy begins. Through his prophet, the Lord will say five times, "With special signs I've been warning you, Israel, yet you do not return to me." You'll find that phrase—"yet you did not return to me" in verses 6, 8, 9, 10, and 11.

What were the warnings?

(1) "I gave you cleanness of teeth in all your cities and lack of bread in all your places," (v. 6). This doesn't mean "Look, mom, no cavities!" Rather it refers to the scarcity of food to get between their teeth in the first place.

(2) "I also withheld the rain from you when there were yet three months to the harvest" (v. 7).

(3) "I smote you with blight and mildew; I laid waste your gardens and your vineyards" (v. 9).

(4) "I slew your young men with the sword." (v. 10) no doubt referring to the difficult wars with Syria.

(5) "I overthrew some of you, as when God overthrew Sodom and Gomorrah, and you were as a brand plucked out of the burning" (v. 11).

I believe Amos is referring to the words of Moses:

When they see the afflictions of that land . . . unsown, and growing nothing, where no grass can sprout, an overthrow like that of Sodom and Gomorrah, . . . yea, all the nations would say, "Why has the Lord done thus to this land?" . . . Then men would say, "It is because they forsook the covenant of the Lord, the God of their fathers, he made with them when he brought them out of the land of Egypt" (Deut. 29: 22-25).

Here are five distinct ways God says to Israel, "I've tried to warn you! "Therefore," he says (v. 12), "thus I will do to you, O Israel; because I will do this to you, prepare to meet your God, O Israel!" Though Amos did not explicitly reveal what God was about to do, when prophets utter, "Prepare to meet your God," it generally means you're about to die, which is exactly what happened to Israel before very long. The nation was obliterated, never to be revived.

Over a hundred years later, Judah, the southern kingdom, would also be conquered, tramp slowly into captivity, but eventually be allowed to return to Jerusalem. But Israel (the ten northern tribes) was so decimated by Assyria that she was referred to ever afterward as the ten *lost* tribes.

Too bad! But then God expects a backslidden people to heed his warning signs. I'll write that again, because that is my key sentence for this chapter. *God expects a backslidden people to heed his warning signs!*

Do you think it's possible that God has been trying to capture backslidden America's ear through such means? If Amos were alive today, might he say, "Five times

God has warned you with obvious signs, America, yet you do not return to him!"

"How?" you ask.

I suggest Amos might respond:

(1) Uncertainty regarding basic oil supplies—or do you not believe God involves himself in such affairs?

(2) Loss of your dollar's value on the international money market.

(3) Loss of prestige throughout the world. Global events now force reevaluation of your once proud self-image.

(4) Even your incredible military power is now in question, because other countries have developed technologies that neutralize what you can or cannot do.

(5) Your stable American way of life is wobbling as inflation makes it increasingly difficult to maintain the standards you knew yesterday and last year. Your leaders admit they're no longer confident they can control it.

In spite of these things you do not return to the Lord. So, having been the richest and most powerful nation in the world, this revelry shall pass away!

While driving on dangerous roads, we expect those responsible for our safety to place signs that warn us of hazards. If notices were not posted we would be angry! Yet we all know that some foolish drivers will speed right by them.

In the spiritual world it is also true that warning signs cannot steer unseeing people to God. Far too often men are like those described in Revelation 16:21. When great hailstones dropped on them, people cursed God for the plague instead of looking to him for help.

I believe these are ominous days in our land. Is it possible we expect state leaders to resolve problems that will not go away apart from a great spiritual awakening because God himself created them?

"Don't be silly, David! It can't be like that!"

I beg your pardon, but to me your comment sounds like something someone might have said to Amos back in Israel around 750 B.C.

Numerous times in my broadcast ministry I have called for prayer for revival. This is not because I think it's a popular message. Rather, I believe God has given me a national pulpit to sound forth this continuous cry—and the time is getting late!

My conviction is that the future of America now rests with the people of God. Whether or not we can extricate ourselves from the self-indulgent life-style that surrounds us, I don't know. But along with my general challenge for revival, the Lord has given me a specific response for which to call. I am seeking people to join together in a Revival Prayer Pact (see at back of book).

What I have in mind involves five basic disciplines: a half-hour every Saturday in private prayer for revival; another quarter hour of prayer before going to church on Sunday for the presence of God to fill his sanctuary; arriving at church fifteen minutes early in an attitude of prayer; reading one book on the topic of revival every three months; and praying once a week with another believer for a great stirring of God across the land.

Some hundreds have joined me in this covenant. It's just a handful, but it's a beginning, and letters reveal God is working powerfully. Hundreds—yes, thousands —more—should respond. Will you be one of those?

4

WHEN GOD GETS MAD
Amos 5—6

Listening to Amos preach in Israel would be an emotional experience. How would you feel if an uninvited foreigner prophesied about your land:

> Fallen, no more to rise, is the virgin Israel; forsaken on her land, with none to raise her up.... The city that went forth a thousand shall have a hundred left, and that which went forth a hundred shall have ten left. ... In all the squares there shall be wailing; and in all the streets they shall say, "Alas! alas!" ... "For I will pass through the midst of you," says the Lord (Amos 5:2, 3, 16-17).

Maybe Amos got away with words like the above simply because the prosperity and strength of the northern kingdom made his threats sound silly. His specific naming of the nation's sins would not have been as easy to swallow. Let's look at random verses from Amos 5 and 6 that focus on themes upon which Amos hammered away.

A key concern was the lack of justice on the part of the leaders, as well as the fact that these people were living in luxury provided by ill-gotten gain.

> For I know how many are your transgressions, and how great are your sins—you who afflict the righteous, who take a bribe (5:12). They hate him who reproves in the gate [the gate was the public place of assembly where tribunals were held], and they abhor him who speaks the truth (v. 10).
>
> Woe to those who lie upon beds of ivory . . . and eat lambs from the flock . . . , who sing idle songs to the sound of the harp, . . . who drink wine in bowls, and anoint themselves with the finest oils (6:4-6).
>
> Woe to those . . . who feel secure on the mountain of Samaria, the notable men of the first of the nations (6:1).
>
> O you who turn justice to wormwood, and cast down righteousness to the earth! . . . Hate evil, and love good, and establish justice in the gate (5:7, 14).

From the record we have of what Amos preached, I presume his delivery was forceful and animated. By trade he was a keeper of trees and a shepherd, so I don't think of him as a polished speaker. What's amazing to me is that he got by with his accusations as long as he did. After all, his home was not Israel but Judah, and the two nations had been separated for close to two hundred years, with enmity between them.

To keep northern people from traveling south to the

temple in Jerusalem, alternate places of worship had been established in Bethel and Dan. There God was represented by golden calves. Jewish law was still honored in Israel and sacrifices made. But this fatal beginning error had resulted in hollow, ritualistic religion and the opening of a door through which all kinds of perversions of worship entered, including the sensual practices of the surrounding peoples.

Here's Amos speaking God's words again:

> I hate, I despise your feasts, and I take no delight in your solemn assemblies. Even though you offer me your burnt offerings and cereal offerings, I will not accept them, and the peace offerings of your fatted beasts I will not look upon. Take away from me the noise of your songs; to the melody of your harps I will not listen. . . . Seek me and live; but do not seek Bethel (Amos 5:21-23, 4-5).

These were strong words with what could easily be interpreted as political overtones.

Let me cover one other area of condemnation in Amos' preaching. There are other accusatory concerns, but these three were his major thrusts: injustice on the part of the leaders, a religion that was profaned, and a lack of compassion for the poor. "You trample upon the poor and take from him exactions of wheat . . . [to get justice the poor were having to pay for it] . . . you have built houses of hewn stone, but you shall not dwell in them; you have planted pleasant vineyards, but you shall not drink their wine" (5:11).

In a study of chapters 5 and 6 of Amos it's obvious that not only was God extremely displeased with Israel, but her doom was sealed as well. Chapter 5 begins, "Hear this word which I take up over you in lamentation, O house of Israel." And chapter 6 ends, "'Behold, I will raise up against you a nation, O house of Israel,' says the Lord, 'and they shall oppress you from the entrance of Hamath to the Brook of the Arabah.'"

Is this judgement of God final, or was there still time to repent? Oddly enough, there's a phrase that appears four times in chapter 5: "Seek me and live" (v. 4) "Seek the Lord and live" (v. 6) "Seek good, and not evil, that you may live; and so the Lord . . . will be with you" (v. 14). "Hate evil, and love good, . . . it may be the Lord, the God of hosts, will be gracious" (v. 15). The key to the future will be the quality of their relationship to God.

"Ah, that dumb Amos! Don't worry about him!" I'm sure some leaders joked. "You don't die as a nation for religious reasons. Crucial to our existence are matters like the economy, and troops for protection, and proper leadership, and law and order, and so on. Keep an eye on Assyria, Damascus and Egypt! That's whom we have to fear. But Jehovah? He's our God!"

Most historians record these ancient events with much the same secular mind-set. What was Israel but another of the small kingdoms swallowed up by the great Assyrian monster? To Amos, however, and the three men who followed him, Hosea, Micah, and Isaiah, destruction would be for one reason only. Israel had gone against the covenant God established with the Hebrew people.

Even now, scholars of this period might laugh and say, "As events unfolded, a national turning toward God really wouldn't have made any difference. Eventually, Assyria would take all in its path anyway. After all, you're talking about the difference between a huge world power and a relatively small kingdom!"

It's interesting to note that about seven years after Israel fell, Hezekiah came to the throne in even smaller Judah (the southern kingdom) and began the process of turning the people there back to the Lord. Read Second Kings 18. In that chapter, Samaria falls after a terrible three-year seige. The predictions Amos made about thirty-five years earlier came true, and now the Assyrians are knocking on the door of Jerusalem. "Pray, speak to your servants in the Aramaic language," yell down the frightened representatives of Hezekiah. "Do not speak to us in the language of Judah within the hearing of the people who are on the wall" (v. 26).

But the tough Assyrian Rabshakeh roars back (v. 27) "Has my master sent me to speak these words to your master and to you, and not to the men sitting on the wall, who are doomed with you to eat their own dung and to drink their own urine?" This blunt talk is a graphic revelation of Assyria's ruthless culture. Without question, these were some of the most cruel invaders of all time.

Do you recall that Hezekiah spread the written demands for surrender out before the Lord? "And that night the angel of the Lord went forth, and slew a hundred and eighty-five thousand in the camp of the Assyrians; and when men arose early in the morning, behold, these were all dead bodies" (2 Kings 19:35).

Which nation was to outlast the other in continuity more than another hundred years? It wasn't powerful Assyria! Rather, it was little Judah, and we know why!

Don't tell Amos that Jehovah's feelings are irrelevant in terms of a nation's survival. To Israel, to Judah, to any people with whom he is displeased, God's message is "Seek me and live!" Now I won't repeat it four times, as Amos did, but this is the theme of this chapter, so let me repeat it once more: *To a people with whom he is disappointed, God's message is "Seek me and live!"*

Is this not something America needs to hear? Just because many think God has been maneuvered into a corner where his role is restricted to mere civil formalities, it doesn't mean he ignores a people who defy his standards of righteousness. He still hates greedy souls who are never satisfied or thankful, even though they have the highest standard of living in the world. He continues to be disgusted when alcohol is consumed by the bowlful, until one is addicted. Always, he's been repelled by people when they chase after every weird cult imaginable. An insatiable appetite for violence in entertainment or reading materials is a sure sign of national godlessness. The Creator knows men can't handle continual sexual stimuli without eventually being consumed by lust. He still hears each time his name is used in vain. Life is far too precious an issue with him to allow abortion to be determined on the casual basis of a woman's personal convenience. Throughout the Scripture God warns that confidence placed in military alliances often proves disappointing! But there's still time. "Seek me and live," he says.

If the majority of America won't hear, possibly those with a true concern for spiritual values will. No doubt judgment can be temporarily stayed even if just that small group responds in time. "Seek God and live!"

But I fear that even many believers do not realize that truly seeking God means a radical departure from contemporary lifestyles. It involves reestablishing priority time with God; no longer excusing long-standing sins; getting rid of elements in a life that inhibit spiritual growth, including (if necessary) twentieth century basics such as television, magazines, newspapers, radios, and so on; developing a new sensitivity to the Holy Spirit's prompting of one's conscience, cultivating a thankful spirit, being concerned about the poor, becoming involved in spiritual warfare, allowing oneself to be broken over lost souls, and certainly, like Amos, wanting justice to roll down like waters and righteousness as an everflowing stream.

5

VISIONS OF
JUDGMENT
Amos 7-9:10

As I attempt to describe the shift that takes place between the material studied to date and the point where chapter 7 begins, you must understand that I have never personally experienced that to which Amos now refers.

In the next two and one-half chapters, he states five times "Thus the Lord God showed me" (Amos 7:1, 4). "He showed me" (v. 7). "Thus the Lord God showed me" (8:1) and "I saw the Lord" (9:1). Now that's different from reporting, "My opinion concerning the future is . . ." or "The other night I dreamed that . . ." or even, "I have a deep anxiety regarding . . ."

I'm probably glad no revelation of this sort has ever come to me. No doubt it would be frightening, especially if each of the visions was distinctly negative. For example, the first of these five revelations begins, "The Lord

God showed me: behold, he was forming locusts in the beginning of the shooting up of the latter growth" (7:1). Now, unlike contemporary newscasters who become accustomed to reporting tragedy without so much as a tremor in their voices, Amos continues after the devastation: "I said, 'O Lord God, forgive, I beseech thee! How can Jacob stand?' . . . The Lord repented concerning this; 'It shall not be,' said the Lord." (7:2-3).

But in a while this divine communication comes again. "Behold, the Lord God was calling for a judgment and it devoured the great deep and was eating up the land. Then I said, 'O Lord God, cease, I beseech thee! How can Jacob stand? He is so small!' . . . 'This also shall not be,' said the Lord God" (vv. 4-6). And the vision ends.

I don't know how many days had passed when, "Behold, the Lord was standing beside a wall . . . with a plumb line in his hand." This is a picture of God testing how true or straight Israel was. "The Lord said, 'Behold, I am setting a plumb line in the midst of my people Israel; I will never again pass by them" (vv. 7-8). He's saying that he won't go by them again without inflicting punishment. "The high places of Isaac shall be made desolate, and the sanctuaries of Israel shall be laid waste, and I will rise against the house of Jeroboam with the sword" (v. 9).

Now let's pause in the narrative for a moment to understand some background. As we've noted before, Amos was a shepherd from the southern kingdom of Judah, sent by the Lord to Israel, the northern kingdom, to warn of judgment because of specific sins. High on the list was the evil an earlier prophet, Elijah, had excoriated, that of following Jehovah plus the deities of the surrounding peoples. Remember how he put it that day on Mount Carmel? "How long will you go limping with two different opinions? If the Lord is God, follow Him; but if Baal, then follow him" (1 Kings 18:21).

This is what the Lord now was talking about in the vision of the plumb line, "The high places [the places of false worship] . . . shall be made desolate."

In chapter 8 Amos returned to the charge of injustice on the part of the leading people, accusing them of dealing deceitfully with false balances, selling the refuse of the wheat, and buying the needy for a pair of sandals (vv. 5-6). In other words, for as small a debt as a pair of sandals, the needy were being condemned to slavery.

That's close to the last of his major criticisms. "Hear this, you who trample upon the needy, and bring the poor of the land to an end" (v. 4).

These were the sins—a mongrel faith, gross injustice, and a callousness toward the poor. Apparently Amos' words were now becoming annoying because Amaziah, the priest of Bethel, tried to scare him off through threats. But we'll save this encounter with Amaziah for another chapter. Right now let's skip to the fourth vision.

"Thus the Lord God showed me: behold, a basket of summer fruit" (8:1). This summer, or ripe, fruit represented Israel as ripe now for judgment. "Then the Lord said to me, 'The end has come upon my people Israel; I will never again pass by them' [he'll no longer allow himself to change his mind]. The songs of the temple shall become wailings in that day . . ., the dead bodies shall be many; in every place they shall be cast out in silence" (vv. 2-3).

Now the final and what must have been the most terrifying vision of all:

I saw the Lord standing beside the altar, and he said; "Smite the capitals until the thresholds shake, and shatter them on the heads of all the people; and what are left of them I will slay with the sword; . . . not one of them shall escape.

Though they dig into Sheol, from there shall my hand take them; though they climb up to heaven, from there I will bring them down. Though they hide themselves on the top of Carmel, from there I will search out and take them; and though they hide from my sight at the bottom of the sea, there will I command the serpent, and it shall bite them. And though they go into captivity before their enemies, there I will command the sword, and it shall slay them; and I will set my eyes upon them for evil and not for good" (9: 1-4).

Frightful words, aren't they? And how terrible to have to pass them on to others with urgency, because before long they would all come true as the bloodthirsty Assyrians conquered the northern kingdom.

Undoubtedly you noticed the progression of severity in these five visions, and also how God became more and more determined to do what was obviously against his desires. Even more fascinating to me, however, is the way punishment was initially forestalled by intercessory prayer on the part of Amos (7:2, 4). "O Lord God, forgive, I beseech thee! How can Jacob stand? He is so small!" And in spite of Israel's years of habitual sinning, the Lord actually yielded to the pleas of Amos twice.

To be sure, a point of no return was reached between visions two and three because God said, "I just can't overlook Samaria's sin any longer" (see 7:8). Yet think, here's a righteous man who knows God is going to punish Israel because of her wickedness, and stirred by the horror of what he sees about to take place, he quickly moves between God and these people to whom he's been preaching so unsuccessfully, and begs the Lord to pity them. He intervenes, or he goes between, which is what intercessory prayer is. It's approaching the Lord on behalf of someone other than yourself. And wonder of wonders—it's unbelievable—the very God of the universe is touched by the concern of Amos and honors it, not just once, but twice!

Which leads me to share my key thought from Amos for this chapter: *National decay can be forestalled in its early stages by the intercessory prayer of God's people.*

I'm hoping some of you are stimulated to question in your minds, "David, do you think it's possible, when a nation takes God's holy name in vain, breaks the principle of the Sabbath, defies his sexual commands, toys with the sacredness of life, where divorce is commonplace, violence dominates all news reports, greed goes unchecked, confidence is ultimately vested in weapons, slavery to alcohol and drugs has reached epidemic proportions, false cults abound, individual entertainment needs now average well over forty hours a week, money dominates people's motives, and God is becoming little more than a vestige of the past—David, do you still think it's possible that a few righteous people could wedge between the scene being described and God and forestall the judgment that's bound to come if things don't change? Do you believe intercessory prayer might work again?"

Yes, it will! I'm convinced of it! But now let me ask you a question. Realizing what's inevitably ahead for any people who defy God, can you be as quickly moved to prayer as Amos was?

Do you know what I think? The fate of this nation rests now in the hands of believers. My personal conviction is that American society in general is traveling so fast on a destruction course that nothing short of another great spiritual awakening is capable of postponing judgment.

But revival of this scope never comes without prevailing prayer. The two always go together.

Probably that's why I sense God has been graciously saying, "Tell my people there's still time. It's late, but you're not yet approaching vision three. To date I haven't yet said, 'Sorry, but I won't be delayed any longer! Never again will I pass by America.' Rather, at the moment I can still be entreated to look with pity on your people and am interested in your thoughts."

6

BUT I THOUGHT GOD PROMISED . . .
Amos 9:11—15

Imagine a conversation between two prosperous men in Israel during the reign of Jeroboam II. By all outward appearances, everything is going extremely well in this northern kingdom.

"Have you been listening to the strange fruit-picker preacher from our neighbor to the south?" asks one.

"Yes," responds the other. "At first I thought he was funny. But now I fear he must soon be silenced, for he lashes out against us and the way we gain our wealth. Dishonest, he says, unjust, and we're trampling on the poor!"

"I wouldn't worry about it my friend," responds the first man. "I hear Amaziah, the head priest at Bethel, plans soon to confront him. And if *you* feel offended, think how angry he must be about the accusations this Amos makes regarding our 'mongrel faith.' Seems he preaches Jehovah is not pleased to share our allegiance with other deities."

"But some of the poor accept his accusations against us!"

"Come now, the man is ignorant and untrained. What influence can he have? Besides, he's now undermined what even the common folks believe. He prophesies total doom for Israel. That's contrary to the promises everyone knows God made. Will Jehovah allow his people to be destroyed? Why just yesterday, he was ranting, 'The Lord says: Israel is no different from the Ethiopians or the Philistines or the Syrians.' Sounds like someone from Judah! Don't worry, my privileged brother, this Amos will soon preach himself into ridicule!"

Well, now, in all his predictions regarding evil days just around the corner, had Amos forgotten God's special relationship to the twelve sons of Jacob? Certainly, it was clear that the Lord had earlier chosen Jacob over the older twin, Esau, and his posterity, Edom. Yet, we're already halfway through chapter 9 in our study, and there is not a single word yet about these unique, long-range blessings, and this is the end of the book.

A study of all these prophets who warned of destruction on behalf of the Lord also reveals a paradoxical theme that states God will remain totally true to his word!

With Amos, this emphasis has been reserved for his finishing flurry! "'Behold, the eyes of the Lord God are upon the sinful kingdom, and I will destroy it from the surface of the ground; except that I will not utterly destroy the house of Jacob. . . . For lo, I will command,

and shake the house of Israel among all the nations as one shakes with a sieve, but no pebble [or kernel] shall fall upon the earth'" (9:8, 9). In other words, just the chaff will be eliminated.

Remember that most of the true worshipers in the north, grieving over the way God had been blatantly symbolized in Israel by a golden calf, had previously emigrated to Judah to be able to worship at the temple in Jerusalem. Thus, even though the people of the north would be so ruthlessly destroyed that they would be referred to as the ten *lost* tribes of Israel, still God says, no kernel (or true follower) shall fall upon the earth.

But warns Amos, "All the sinners of my people shall die by the sword, who say, 'Evil shall not overtake or meet us'" (9:10). God's promises are always true. It's just that they are conditional.

Most parents can relate to this: "We'll go to the zoo Saturday if you kids keep your things picked up." If all week their rooms look like the city dump, you're not going to be intimidated from saying, "Sorry, but the trip's off!"

"But you promised us!" they'll whine. Sure you did, but your children have forgotten something.

Most of God's promises are reserved for those who remain faithful to him! His agreements are made invalid by gross disobedience.

"Hey, wait a minute!" someone protests. "If that's the case, how come we still expect God to act on Israel's behalf?" A fast answer—partly because of oaths God also made to unusually righteous *individuals* like Abraham and David, that he's going to keep. Believe me, God knows how to reward the faithful.

In that day I will raise up the booth of David that is fallen [the southern kingdom of Judah, David's tribe would also fall, but it would not be eradicated like Israel] and repair its breeches, and raise up its ruins, and rebuild it as in the days of old; that they may possess the remnant of Edom [Esau's offspring] and all the nations who are called by my name" (9:11-12).

When you have time, look up Acts 15 and you'll find James, the leader of the New Testament church in Jerusalem, quoting this passage ("and all the nations who are called by my name") as a reason for receiving Gentile converts into the body.

Scholars generally agree, however, that the promises in verses 11-15 go beyond Judah's return from exile. Again note that I said "Judah." Israel, the northern kingdom, didn't go into exile. People of that nation, for all practical purposes, were either exterminated or assimilated.

Relating to the theme of God's great promises, Amos now looks down the years to the time of the arrival of the great son of David. And even further than that, he sees a day when this Messiah will reign in power.

"Behold, the days are coming," says the Lord, "when the plowman shall overtake the reaper and the treader of grapes him who sows the seed; the mountains shall drip sweet wine, and all the hills shall flow with it. I will restore the fortunes of my people Israel, and they shall rebuild the ruined cities and inhabit them; they shall plant vineyards and drink their wine, and they shall make gardens and eat their fruit. I will plant them upon their land, and they shall never again be plucked up out of the land which I have given them," says the Lord your God (vv. 13-15).

All this will come true. God's promises are valid. Of course, modern Israel must first acknowledge her true Lord!

We have come to the end of our initial survey of Amos, but we still have three passages that need further exploring.

Whole sections of Scripture like these come alive because in many ways the life of Israel has been the story of every nation, even every man. The downward pull is strong within us all. These prophetic warnings are always appropriate somewhere. In this day I believe they are pregnant with meaning for Americans, where conversations such as the following might be all too typical.

"What irritates me is every time something goes wrong for us in the world, the crazy preachers interpret it as God's warning to us about judgment for sin."

"Come on, they're part of the scene. They help make American culture colorful."

"Forget it, it's not colorful when your wife starts being affected by such talk. Last week she asked me if I thought maybe we could start living more simply. Fine—but next thing I find she's been helping this poor family across town!"

"Really? Well I wouldn't worry—Americans are success-oriented. Too much soberness and soon the guys you're talking about won't have enough donations to keep preaching. What religious people in the States like to hear about is how God's going to bless them. Listen to the ministers who really have a following and you'll see I'm right. "'God loves you,' they say, 'Something nice awaits you around the corner.' 'Jesus wants to help you see your dreams come true!' Now those guys know the secret to bigness and longevity. So just sit it out, Max. The small brimstone boys can't stay around too long!"

Actually there's a place for both truths, blessing and judgment. For those who are faithful (people/nations), there is no better life than following hard after God, because He can't be outgiven. It is also true, as Jonathan Edwards appropriately preached years ago, that sinners in the hands of an angry God have much to fear.

The job of ministers is to determine the mind of the Lord as it relates to a given individual, congregation, or nation, and then to share what is most fitting. Whereas it's inappropriate to preach a steady diet of judgment to faithful saints, so it's equally out of line to parade God's wondrous promises before those who long ago abandoned their first love.

I'm certain Amos did not enjoy being harsh, nor had he forgotten God's goodness. Rather, he was divinely compelled to speak what was appropriate to his setting. So must all who are truly called by God.

The material I have chosen to underscore by writing this book reveals my prayerful analysis of the day.

7

A GREAT DAY IS COMING
Amos 5:18-20

A belief that someday God is going to intervene in history and set everything right is not a new hope.

In several of his sermons Amos talks about the coming day of the Lord. Apparently, his listeners were familiar with the term, because he didn't explain it at all. In fact, in chapter 5 Amos referred to people who wanted this day of the Lord to come.

"Good for them!" you say. Not really, and in a moment I'll explain why.

First, though, let's paint a little more background. During this period of history I'm sure the established families of Israel would have evaluated the state of their nation as very good. The long reign of Jeroboam II had resulted in prosperity and military strength unlike any period since the days of Solomon.

Ethically and morally, however, the nation was definitely in need of a prophet's visit. It was common knowledge that the wealthy had taken advantage of the rest of the population. Through bribes they insured the determination of judicial decisions. For as small a debt as a pair of sandals, those unable to pay their creditors were condemned to slavery! False balances were used in business. Robbery and violence were not uncommon. Three times Amos would say accusingly, "You trample the head of the poor into the dust" (see 2:7, 5:11, 8:4).

Other evils of that time included drunkenness, unchecked lust, and a small elitist element living like kings in extreme luxury, with no conscience at all about the poor.

A further factor that made an outside voice necessary if a word was to again be heard from the Lord, was that spiritually the kingdom was close to bankruptcy. "Here is your God who delivered you from Egypt," the people had been told, when golden calves were first unveiled at their two national religious centers (see 2 Kings 10:29). Through the years, this initial error would be the opening through which would pour literally all kinds of religious perversions. Even the appearance of earlier spiritual giants, such as Elijah and Elisha, had not been enough to offset the apostasy.

Not that Jehovah had been forsaken. Most of the people of Israel not only saw him as their principle deity, but actually practiced faithfully the ceremonial forms that had been handed down. Yet it was all hollow ritual.

"God says, 'I hate, I despise your feasts, and I take no delight in your solemn assemblies,'" boomed Amos (5:21). "Even though you offer me your burnt offerings and cereal offerings, I will not accept them, and the peace offerings of your fatted beasts I will not look upon. Take away from me the noise of your songs; to the melody of your harps I will not listen. But let justice roll down like waters, and righteousness like an everflowing stream" (5:21-24).

Possibly you understand now why Amos was not impressed that certain people in Israel wanted the day of the Lord to arrive. In spite of the fact that their faith had minimal bearing on how they lived, they claimed these promises as part of their national heritage, and apparently certain worshipers maintained great confidence in them. After all, was not the day of Jehovah the time when God would avenge his people of all their enemies and fully restore their fortunes?

Woe to you who desire the day of the Lord! Why would you have the day of the Lord? It is darkness, and not light; as if a man fled from a lion, and a bear met him; or went into the house and leaned with his hand against the wall, and a serpent bit him. Is not the day of the Lord darkness, and not light, and gloom with no brightness in it (5:18).

The picture Amos paints here hardly points to the day of the Lord as being the cure-all certain Israelites anticipated. That's not to say such momentous events contained no positive implications. We've already studied the last half of chapter 9. "In that day I will raise up the booth of David that is fallen" (v. 11). Remember? "Behold, the days are coming when the plowman shall overtake the reaper, . . . and the treader of grapes him who sows the seed" (v. 13). So the element of national exaltation was not eliminated.

Yet Amos warns that the day of the Lord, those catastrophic times when the very God of the universe steps directly into the affairs of man, will also involve unexpected dread. Good news, Israel; you outran the lion. Bad news; you ran smack into a bear! Good news; you miraculously escaped the bear and found the shelter of your home. Bad news; you leaned against the wall to rest and a poisonous serpent sank his fangs into your arm!

So, good news—yes! The promise of a day of the Lord ahead is yours. But bad news as well. For this generation it is all gloom with no brightness in it. Thoughts about the coming great day of the Lord should be tempered by soberness. Because our historical perspective allows us to know a little of the carnage that took place when Israel fell to the Assyrians, these foretellings were undoubtedly understatements!

Do you have the uncanny feeling that this unlearned shepherd and dresser of sycamore trees might have liked a chance to speak to *us?*

"America! God is displeased with your empty mottos. Beware lest you, too, live on the waning spiritual momentum of previous generations. You who think of yourselves as champions of justice, why is it you are so despised around the world? Even while your craving for more of the finest of everything goes unchecked, powerful enemies are carefully plotting your demise. You arm your allies only to watch them point their new weapons in your direction. Your lust is epidemic; violence marks your national personality, false cults abound, you legitimatize your outlawed gambling, you kill what you yourselves conceive, you consume alcohol by the tubful, you take God's name in vain, you dilute the Sabbath, the songs in your mouths are filthy, by saying, 'After all, not everyone has the same preference,' you even presume you can make sodomy vanish!"

"And to you who follow the religion of your forefathers —rather than influencing your society as you should, tragically it has the stronger lure on your emotions. You fraternize with its gods of lust and money and status. Hear the Lord speak: 'The stench of broken marriage vows in the church offends my nostrils! How shamefully indiscriminate my people are in what they read and listen to and laugh at. You say you have no time for the physically poor, or the spiritually deprived, though you waste hours watching trivia—both secular and religious. Glutted with knowledge, you seek deeper spiritual insight and don't even yet perceive you're involved in a great war between light and darkness, the ways of life and those of death, truth and deceit, your God and Satan.'

"'But no. You're casual about the church and you stifle the convicting work of my Holy Spirit. Confession no longer interests you. Craving present acceptance, you're apprehensive about the future and for conversation say hopefully, "Must not the day of the Lord be coming soon now?" Why would you want the day of the Lord?'"

"Could it be your thinking is confused, my friends?" Amos might continue. "Like some in ancient Israel, might your expectations be different than reality? Maybe the promise you have in mind will prove valid for a generation yet to come, and your day to meet God as a nation is darkness and not light, gloom with no brightness in it. After all, it wouldn't be the first time in history a backslidden people were thus deceived. Be warned, then, lest your naivete be your ruin. Thoughts about the coming great day of the Lord should be tempered by soberness!"

This key sentence seems so obvious when referring to Amos' message to Israel. *Thoughts about the coming great day of the Lord should be tempered by soberness.* When God takes matters into his own hands at any occasion, it is not a time about which you want to be ill-informed. For the sinful, the day of the Lord always means judgment.

Yet, an exclusive negative posture can become depressive, so let's look at a more positive stance on the same subject from the pen of Peter.

Therefore gird up your minds, be sober, set your hope fully upon the grace that is coming to you at the revelation of Jesus Christ. As obedient children, do not be conformed to the passions of your former ignorance, but as he who called you is holy, be holy yourselves in all your conduct; since it is written, "You shall be holy, for I am holy." And if you invoke as Father him who judges each one impartially according to his deeds, conduct yourselves with fear throughout the time of your exile (1 Pet. 1:13-17).

Thus Peter, centuries after Amos, echoes one of his themes, and it is subject material we of the twentieth century should to contemplate: Thoughts about the coming great day of the Lord should be tempered by soberness.

8

A VITAL NATIONAL RESOURCE
Amos 7:10-17

A good act is hard to follow. Think how Amos must have felt, since his immediate prophetic predecessors were Elijah, Elisha, and Jonah.

About a hundred years earlier on Mount Carmel, the first of this illustrious trio had prayed down fire from heaven. Then, lo and behold, a double portion of Elijah's spirit rested on miracle-working Elisha, whose deeds were no doubt still vividly remembered by the oldest citizens in Israel. And what prophet could match the even more recent hair-raising account of Jonah and the incredible success of his preaching mission at Nineveh, capital of the ruthless Assyrians?

So now, what evidence would Amos have to offer as to his authenticity? Actually, his credentials were nothing more than an awareness that God had called him from his simple chores in Judah to travel north to Israel and warn of divine judgment unless they repented.

Not content with generalities, Amos had zeroed in on specific sins. "You trample the head of the poor into the dust of the earth," Amos would repeat again and again. "Woe to you!" Denunciations were also forthcoming against the religious practices of the nation. Continuing to carefully observe the forms of Judaism, Israel had again taken to the forbidden practices of the surrounding peoples. Figuring they had better keep all the gods happy, this foolish generation now even involved itself in the fertility rites of the pagans!

"A man and his father go in to the same maiden [or cult prostitute], so that my holy name is profaned" (2:7).

"Even though you offer me your burnt offerings and cereal offerings, I will not accept them" (5:22).

The theme of Amos was that because of these and other evils, judgment would soon be forthcoming. "The high [idolatrous] places of Isaac shall be made desolate, and the sanctuaries of Israel shall be laid waste, and I will rise against the house of Jeroboam with the sword" (7:9).

"Then Amaziah, the priest of Bethel [one of the two northern "holy cities"] sent to Jeroboam king of Israel, saying, 'Amos has conspired against you in the midst of the house of Israel; the land is not able to bear all his words'" (7:10).

Amaziah spoke to Amos: "'O seer, go, flee away to the land of Judah, and eat bread there, and prophesy there; but never again prophesy at Bethel, for it is the king's sanctuary, and it is a temple of the kingdom'" (v. 12).

In general, people don't like to hear what prophets

have to say. In fact, Amos had already charged, "You . . . commanded the prophets saying, 'You shall not prophesy'" (2:12).

A few years later Hosea will report a similar response to his words. "'The prophet is mad,' Israel protests, 'this inspired fellow is raving.'—Ah yes, but only because your iniquity is so great, your apostasy so grave" (Hos. 9:7, JB).

"One should not preach of such things, disgrace will not overtake us" (Mic. 2:6). That's Micah, recording the people's reaction to him. It's the same time frame. Micah and Isaiah preach in Judah, but their statements apply to Israel as well. "If a man should go about and utter wind and lies," Micah continues (2:11), "saying, 'I will preach to you of wine and strong drink, he would be the preacher for this people!'"

Here's Isaiah, the last of the four who lived during the period of Israel's great fall. "For they are a rebellious people, lying sons, sons who will not hear the instruction of the Lord; who say to the seers, 'See not'; and to the prophets, 'Prophesy not to us what is right; speak to us smooth things, prophesy illusions'" (30:9-10).

Apparently, it's common to not want to hear your sins enumerated through a man like this whose biting words are made even more pointed by the inner voice of God's convicting spirit.

Yet nation's destinies are determined by how God's prophets are received. May I write that again? *Nations' destinies are determined by how God's prophets are received.*

Had not Nineveh (Assyria) been spared when its king called his people to don sackcloth and fast following

Jonah's sober messages? Much later, an opposite response would be offered by the Jews to One far greater than Jonah. Do you recall the words of our Lord? "O Jerusalem, Jerusalem, killing the prophets and stoning those who are sent to you!" Because they received even a perfect prophet in such fashion, the following judgment was pronounced, "Behold, your house is forsaken and desolate" (Matt. 37-38).

So it was also to be in the northern kingdom of Israel. Speaking through Amos, Hosea, Micah, and Isaiah, God was rebuking his people loudly and clearly! "Beware, Israel! danger lurks just ahead! How you receive what we as revealers of God's mind have to share is up to you, but we have no choice but to deliver our messages."

This explains why Amos responded as he did to Amaziah's command to flee to Judah and never again prophesy at Bethel. Amos was not paid to speak:

I am no prophet, [in other words, I'm not clergy who works for pay like you do] nor a prophet's son; but I am a herdsman, and a dresser of sycamore trees, and the Lord took me from following the flock, and the Lord said to me, "Go prophesy to my people Israel."

Now therefore hear the word of the Lord. You say, "Do not prophesy against Israel, and do not preach against the house of Isaac." Therefore thus says the Lord: "Your wife shall be a harlot in the city, and your sons and your daughters shall fall by the sword, and your land shall be parceled out by line; you yourself shall die in an unclean land, and Israel shall surely go into exile away from its land" (Amos 7:14-17).

We don't know what actually happened to Amaziah and his family, but judging from the accuracy of the predictions Amos made regarding Jeroboam and the fate of the nation, I think I can venture a pretty safe guess. Within six months of the death of the king, his dynasty was destroyed, and before another thirty years had passed, the nation of Israel was no more!

Granted, no miracles, fire from heaven, or deliverance from the belly of a great fish validated Amos' claim to speak for God. Nevertheless, the message he faithfully discharged on God's behalf carried considerable clout! His prophecies were fulfilled.

Are you one who believes history repeats itself? Could it be that in our time people still become uneasy when voices are raised in warning as to the deteriorating health of a nation?

Doesn't God declare that land, which at one time knew few divorces, to be in serious trouble when a new generation now decides just to live together without marriage? When the average seventeen-year-old American has witnessed 18,000 murders on tv, why be amazed that violence dominates the news? If changes are mostly for the worse, does it take a genius to predict trouble ahead? What fool will someday stand before a holy God and claim the current raging flood of pornography in this country helped improve its sexuality? Is more than common sense required to understand the Creator's attitude concerning abortion under normal circumstances, when his very attributes include life, not death. Does it not seem peculiar that gambling was thought unlawful until the government saw in it a way to cover its inability to stop spending more money than it collected? But praise God! today's headlines tell of revival! Wait—not of the church—but of Islam!

"Hey, preacher!" a voice interrupts. "Get wise! If you want people to support you—start saying what they want to hear, like 'Something good is coming your way!' 'Your fondest dreams will undoubtedly come true if you have faith.' 'Good buddy, God wants you to enjoy the blessings of this world in abundance!'"

Amaziahs and Amoses. God help us in this land to know the difference between them.

Poor Israel didn't! As you hear these last words from Amos, reflect on how long they have remained true regarding Israel.

"Behold, the days are coming" says the Lord God, "when I will send a famine on the land; not a famine of bread, or a thirst for water, but of hearing the words of the Lord. They shall wander from sea to sea, and from north to east; they shall run to and fro, to seek the word of the Lord, but they shall not find it" (8:11-12).

May it never be reported that the Lord no longer speaks in America!

9

A WORD TO WOMEN
Amos 4:1-3

Hindsight is usually better than foresight. Had ancient Israel known around 760 or 770 B.C. that not many years hence it would be totally obliterated, I'm sure its people would have been greatly alarmed. At the moment, however, the nation's leaders must have felt things could hardly have been going better. And did anyone of rank seriously notice the public preaching of that southerner from Judah? "Ha, ha, you mean that simple shepherd or dresser of sycamore trees—which was it now?"

According to Amos, God was greatly upset. "God has said judgment is just ahead!" he warned. But apparently, his indictments bothered very few.

I wonder, though, if several decades later, the voice of the prophet didn't come back to haunt many during those three long years when Samaria was under Assyrian siege? Certainly they knew that these conquerors (noted above all else for their cruelty) could be counted on to show little pity to a state that, following Jeroboam's death, had sworn allegiance, paid tribute, and then attempted to squirm out from under their pledge.

When it was all over, there was no more northern kingdom of Israel. Either exterminated or taken captive, the nation and its people died a violent death.

For a final look at Amos, I'd like to return to chapter 4 where he addressed the moneyed wives of the kingdom. His words there in verses 1-3 are directed specifically to the female elite, a small number because most women in that culture were nobodys. Not to be a male was to suffer numerous social injustices.

Now here were some women who knew not only prejudice but also privilege! They were in-between, neither-nors. Should they not, then, be able to identify with the suffering of those who were less fortunate and serve as a check on their insensitive, power-hungry husbands? Could they not speak words like, "My dear, does not our law require that a poor man's coat taken in pledge be returned to him at sundown? But you have kept it! Why?" In most cases, those who have known oppression often have a greater sense of justice.

This has to be what Amos hoped to find regarding the wealthy wives in Samaria. But, no! I'll let him speak:

Hear this word, you cows of Bashan [that's a geographic area noted for its well-fed cattle], . . . who oppress the poor, who crush the needy, who say to their husbands, "Bring, that we may drink!" The Lord God has sworn by his holiness that, behold, the days are coming upon you, when they shall take you away with hooks.

Unfortunately, what Amos discovered were privileged women—women with time, money, influence, and greater knowledge; women of religious heritage—but women who were self-centered, insensitive to the suffering all around them, and stupid regarding unfolding events that would soon cost them all the advantages they possessed.

"Hey, dear, bring me another drink!" What a sad commentary when so much was at stake!

It's a foreboding sign when a nation's elevated women become hardened and tough. On the other hand, I believe *privileged women who are godly can protect a nation from destruction.*

Much later, the exiled people of southern Judah would see this cause and effect displayed in startling fashion when Esther, beautiful spiritually as well as physically, was the queen of Ahasuerus of Persia. Her obedient godliness preserved her people from genocide.

Such a truth is appropriate for our day as well. I'm presupposing, of course, that God still becomes angry with nations that stray from him. Not that America ever was Christian per se. But at least in past generations the standard of right or wrong certainly was more consistent with the teachings of Scripture than now.

Divorce was not nearly so common. Magazines featuring male and female nudity and all manner of perversions were not sold in the corner drugstore. Murders didn't fill page after page of news copy. Hard work was a virtue and no one dreamed a man or his neighbor would someday be entertained via television an average of forty three hours a week. The Lord's Day was respected even by merchants. Cults were a fringe element. Profanity was banned on the national media. No one talked of equal rights for homosexuals. Few took astrology seriously. Public prayer was expected at most functions. Virginity was a virtue. Unless it was a most exceptional case, abortion was not even considered an option because life was viewed as sacred. And few predicted gambling would be sponsored by the government, and maybe some day prostitution!

Am I making my point?

No, America has never come close to being the Kingdom of God, but of late the gap has been widening at an incredible and alarming rate. I fear, like ancient Israel, we may not realize in all our talk about possible enemies that the worst of all powers to be pitted against us is the Lord!

One way our land differs from this Old Testament account is in the greater percentage of privileged women. Oh, I realize it remains a man's world as far as many advantages are concerned, but the women of history would undoubtedly see this time and place as one of their finest hours.

Because those who experience discrimination are generally more sensitive to right and wrong, they become an instrument by which to measure the whole of a given society. If most of these privileged women live for self—"I want this, bring me that!"—or are insensitive to others' pains; if they never identify with the poor, the sick, or even so much as say a prayer for the millions of this world's starving children; if they go through this day with no thought that tomorrow may not be moneyed or enjoyable or peaceful; then we are indeed far down the road of no return. "Fat cows of Bashan!"

Maybe to such a group today an Amos would shout, "Sad, comic Miss Piggys wrapped up in self, shielded from the unseemly by your world of luxury, conscious only of the busy present—beware! When advantaged women become hardened, they speed a nation toward its doom."

Because I know that godly women serve as a great bastion of defense against the powers of evil, I rejoice today in what I observe happening among so many of my sisters in the faith. Not content to allow a setting of plenty to spoil you, your pursuit of God is marked by increased time in his presence. You hunger to know more of the Word, your prayer life is maturing, you are developing the discipline of a tender conscience toward the Holy Spirit.

What you're doing is right! I applaud your efforts, I encourage you to be brave even if the way is lonely. I'm thankful for your numbers. I affirm again your importance. Like Mordecai of old, I remind you (Esther 4:14), "Who knows whether you have not come to the kingdom for such a time as this?"

As brothers who through the years have had more opportunities and encouragement along such lines, we notice and rejoice, and pledge ourselves anew because of your example, to the task at hand.

I pray in King David's words (Psalm 144:12-15):

May our sons in their youth be like plants full grown, our daughters like corner pillars cut for the structure of a palace; may our garners be full, providing all manner of store; . . . may there be no cry of distress in our streets! Happy the people to whom such blessings fall! Happy the people whose God is the Lord!

Is that not the final promise of Amos as well?

Seek good, and not evil, that you may live; and so the Lord God of hosts, will be with you. . . . "The mountains shall drip sweet wine, and all the hills shall flow with it. I will restore the fortunes of my people Israel, and they shall rebuild the ruined cities and inhabit them; they shall plant vineyards and drink their wine, and they shall make gardens and eat their fruit. I will plant them upon their land, and they shall never again be plucked up out of the land which I have given them,' says the Lord your God (5:14, 9:13-15).

Sisters and brothers, together let us be people in whom God takes delight.

REVIVAL PRAYER PACT

With God's enabling, by faith, I promise . . .

1. to spend one-half hour every Saturday in private prayer for revival.

2. to devote one-quarter hour each Sunday (before going to church if at all possible) in private prayer for revival.

3. to make plans to arrive at church (or Sunday school) fifteen minutes before the scheduled starting time in order to be in a prayerful attitude regarding these meetings.

4. to pray once a week specifically for revival with at least one other believer.

5. to average reading one book on the topic of revival every three months. (I understand I can choose to end my commitment to this prayer pact when twelve books on revival have been studied.)

Signature _____
　　　　　　　　　　　　Date

I have this day committed myself to the Revival Prayer Pact.

Signature _____ Date_____

Name _____ Address_____

_____
City   State   Zip

Pastor_____

Church_____ Address_____

_____
City   State   Zip

Send to: The Chapel of the Air, Inc.,
           Wheaton, Illinois 60187